This book has been published in association with the
Christian Evidence Society. The Society has existed
since 1870 to present the fundamental truths of
Christianity to enquirers. Its address is:

1 Little Cloister
Westminster Abbey
London
SW1P 3PL

Other titles in this series:

Why God?
Why Pray?
Why Suffering?
Finding God in Later Life
Finding God in Bereavement
Finding God in Illness
Finding God in Marriage Breakdown

Why Belief?

Richard Holloway

CHRISTIAN
EVIDENCE
SOCIETY

LION PUBLISHING

Copyright © 1993 Richard Holloway
The author asserts the moral right to be identified as the
author of this work

This edition published in 1997 by Lion Publishing plc Sandy
Lane West, Oxford, England
ISBN 0 7459 3712 8

Albatross Books Pty Ltd PO Box 320, Sutherland, NSW 2232,
Australia
ISBN 0 7324 1587 X

First edition 1997
10 9 8 7 6 5 4 3 2 1 0

Jesus said to him, 'Do you believe because you see me? How happy are those who believe without seeing me!'

John 20:29

Why Belief?

What is belief?

We must begin by noting that belief is not knowledge. When we use the word knowledge we normally use it to mean something that has been proved to be the case. The process that leads to what we call factual knowledge is usually by a method called induction. By observing particular situations we develop generalizations that we call knowledge of fact.

Most of the multiplication tables are of this sort. We observe that two plus two adds up to four; and we can prove this by placing two lots of two apples on the table in front of us. So the claim that two plus two equals four is a fact of knowledge, something that can be proved by demonstration.

But it's not always as simple as that. We know that observers often see things differently. A story from the University of Moscow will illustrate this.

A professor used to arrange for someone to rush into his room during a lecture and start a fight. After the thug was ejected the professor would ask his students what they had observed. The observations were all different. Some students saw not one thug but two. The professor would conclude the demonstration by pointing out that it illustrated an ancient Roman proverb, 'to lie like an eye-witness'. The observer affects what is seen and observers sometimes see different things, so we should always tinge our most solid convictions with a certain reserve of scepticism. Nevertheless, we have to give words a general use and for most purposes there is a distinction between knowledge and belief. Most of us use knowledge to describe tested fact, something that has been *proved* to be the case.

What, then, is belief? Belief is not certain knowledge that a thing is the case, but trust that it is the case. We cannot demonstrate its mathematical reality the way we can test the two-times table with a bag of apples. It is something that commends itself to us in a way that captures our trust in the absence of proof.

Belief, of course, is not indifferent to knowledge. Indeed, intimate knowledge of someone over the years is likely to lead us to trust that person in situations of possible doubt. But there is always an element of risk involved because the person may not turn out to be worthy of our belief after all. If we reflect upon it, we can see that all the important human relationships are based on trust, not knowledge; instinct, not proof; intuition, not demonstration. Over the years, of course, our belief is validated by the faithfulness of the person we have trusted. But the whole essence of belief or trust (in many ways a better word to describe the same experience) lies in the area where proof is not possible. In these situations where action is demanded without certain knowledge of the outcome, we either hold back in fear or mistrust or go forward in faith. We know that there are many tragic people who are chronically mistrustful, incapable of committing themselves to others, always suspicious and holding back. Some have been so wounded by their early experiences that they constantly demand from those who love them evidence or proof of that love in a way that is impossible to give. People like this find trust difficult, if not impossible.

All of this goes to show that trust or belief is a fundamental element in normal human relationships. It is also an essential element in personal development. We must learn to trust others if we would be truly human. We must also learn to trust ourselves if we are to grow in our own humanity. This self-trust can be used in a cheap, huckstering sort of way, to make us better at selling ourselves, what they call the power of positive thinking. Nevertheless, it is an important element in human dignity. We must have some confidence in ourselves before tackling important and demanding tasks because we can never know in advance how we are going to do.

Even a superficial meditation on the subject shows us how fundamental belief is to human life in all sorts of areas. In most human relationships and in personal development, belief in others and the kind of belief in ourselves we think of as appropriate self-confidence are absolute requirements if we are to relate to others, grow in those relationships and develop our own humanity to its fullest potential.

What is the opposite of belief?

The opposite of belief is not, as many people suppose, doubt, but distrust, the inability to put ourselves into someone else's hands, to trust ourselves to their responsibility. The opposite of trust is a kind of moral impotence or fear that traps us and imprisons us, making action impossible. We stand indecisively on the window-ledge of the burning building because we are afraid that the firemen below us, who are calling us to jump, will not really be able to save us. We have to trust them in order to live. The drowning swimmer, in a frenzy of anxiety, has to trust the life-saver and relax into her arms if he wants to be pulled safely to the beach. The apprentice rock climber has to believe that the guide will hold him on the ropes if he falls off a difficult face, or he will never make even a beginning as a climber. We cannot prove in advance the outcome of these situations. We cannot live beyond all these accumulated moments of anxiety to see that all will be well. We have to make acts of trust. Without trust or belief there would be no action, no doing of anything.

We would never get on a bus, a train or an aeroplane without belief. We would never accept another person's word or commit ourselves to a surgeon's knife. Life is a network of relationships that require our trust.

And doubt is an inescapable element in the human experience of belief. In the absence of proof there will always, *must* always be doubt. Another way of putting this is to say that human beings live with anxiety. We live in an uncertain universe in which many tragedies occur, but doubt or anxiety, though they accompany belief, do not essentially contradict it. In fact, without doubt or anxiety there could be no trust. It is precisely those situations that make us anxious that call for trust. One of the lessons of life is that while practice never makes perfect, it does make the doing of a thing better and more confident, less anxious. Like everything else, faith takes practice, which is one reason why modern psychotherapy sometimes makes use in group work of trust games, in which people are taught to fall backwards into the arms of others, to learn the lesson of trust and commitment to their care.

One of the greatest of human

tragedies is the evolution of the person who is incapable of human trust. This is usually a result of the experience of betrayal in precisely those relationships that call for the most basic and essential elements of trust. If our parents betray us by abusing us, if our leaders betray us by exploiting us for their own gratification or enlargement, then chronic mistrust is bred in us and we become cynics. The cynic is the direct opposite of the person of faith. The word cynic comes from the Greek word for dog, and it refers to the kind of person who is always snapping or whining, complaining or savaging some ideal or human reality. Cynics trust nothing and no one, and they end up trapped inside their own heads, gripped in the relentless pain of chronic disbelief. They have become people who are incapable of living contentedly in the universe as it is, because ours is a universe that demands trust if we are to flourish as human beings, developing and growing in commitment not only to ourselves and to others, but to the whole human and global enterprise. If we refuse the risk of trust, we will be stranded on the bank forever, like the son of the woman who said that she wouldn't let her little Jimmy into the water until he learned to swim.

But why believe in God?

Now we have to jump a gear. Maybe we are a little clearer about the role of belief in ordinary human affairs, but why believe in God? What difference does that kind of trust make? Putting questions in this way makes it all sound like some kind of profit or benefit system: you show me what profit or benefit believing in God will produce and I'll believe; tell me what I'll get out of it and I'll trust God. This is not what we do in healthy human relationships. We don't trust in others in order to benefit or profit ourselves. We trust because it is our nature to enter commitments, to put our trust in people.

Childhood and parenthood are the best examples of this. This is why abusive parents are so unnatural, we feel, so destructive of the web of human trust. In other words, trust is an endowment, a gift, something that is simply given to us. We find that we do trust our parents, we do trust our leaders, we do trust the fireman who tells us to jump. We know there are untrustworthy parents, but we also know that trust is the very basis of human community. This is why the contradiction or betrayal of these relationships that require basic trust is so unspeakable, so contrary to what ought to be the case that it makes us mad just to contemplate it. We say of parents who sexually abuse their children, 'we just can't believe it'. These basic relationships of trust have a kind of sacred givenness about them. We believe that parents ought to be trustworthy carers of their children, and that leaders should not betray their people because, without trust, human relating becomes impossible and we fall into a kind of insanity. It is not a matter of profit or benefit. It is, we might say, a matter of nature, something given and self-evidently good, without which we cannot be human at all.

All of this is also true of belief or trust in God. This kind of trust is a fact of human experience long before it is used or abused by humanity for other ends or purposes. There have been several attempts in recent years to prove that belief in God is not like basic human trust, but is something much more calculating and unhealthy. The main criticism is that belief is used as an instrument for gaining other ends. Far from being a basic instinct, it is something artificial and self-conscious. The most famous of these accounts of faith came from Sigmund Freud and Karl Marx. Freud taught that belief is a consolation mechanism. We project our own fear and loneliness onto the blank screen of the universe and bounce back a comforting fairytale that tells us we are not alone. Marx's point of view was characteristically different, seeing belief as a temporary consolation for the miseries of life, which is cruelly manipulated by those in power to hold humanity in subjection. Now it is obvious that belief, like anything human, can be and almost certainly will be abused and turned to wrong uses. But that is not what Freud and Marx are saying. They are saying that the origin of belief itself comes from our fear and loneliness. The trouble with claims of this sort is that they are unprovable, since the origin of faith lies back in the mists of time.

Freud and Marx are guilty of a common human failing, which is to read their own conclusions back into time and see them as originating explanations. We might as well argue that children trust their parents because they are comforted thereby and that parents encourage such trust because they are able to use it as a means of control and manipulation. Doubtless there are particular instances where the diseased version of human trust is the case, but it cannot account for human trust in itself and seems contrary to basic human experience. We trust because we trust.

We have already seen that belief is one of the fundamental structures of our humanity. In intellectual history, theories always follow and invariably to some extent distort the experience they try to describe. Human beings find themselves believing. They have a primary trust in life and in others.

We can analyse it away. It can be eroded in the way that any relationship can be destroyed, but these are diseases that do not invalidate the healthy state.

In many ways, ours is a self-consciously cynical era that takes considerable pleasure in debunking and reducing the reputations of people. This kind of cynicism is a self-destructive parasite in the human system which is capable of eroding and destroying all trust. This is one reason why people in our society are reluctant to talk about matters of faith, because they fear the challenge of the cynical debunker.

Nevertheless, the facts suggest that this primary trust or belief is an almost universal human instinct. Survey after survey shows that most people have an instinctive belief in God and many of them claim to have had personal experiences of the divine.

Believing *in* and believing *that*

There is an ancient and useful distinction that we should note between believing *in* something and believing *that* something is the case. Believing that something is the case need not require commitment or personal response from us. For instance, I believe that Mount Everest is the highest mountain in the world, because I have been told so by people who understand these things and whose opinions I trust. But believing that Mount Everest is the highest mountain in the world makes absolutely no difference to my life. And believing *that* God exists can be equally neutral in its effect. St James tells us that even the devils believe that God exists. So believing *that* God is, which most people apparently do, is a fact of not very great significance since it may be no more than a piece of mental furniture. Believing *in* a thing, on the other hand, involves action, the kind of action that characterizes relationships based on trust.

The consequences of believing in God

What, then, are the effects of believing *in* God, or having an experience of God that causes us to put our trust in the divine mystery? There seem to be three main elements in the experience, that continue to characterize the relationship of trust in the divine mystery we call God. The most characteristic thing about believers in God is that they *worship* God according to their uses and traditions. This seems to be the primary impulse. Whenever a human experiences or meets the divine mystery, the instinct is to fall down and worship, to give worth to the mystery perceived. This was Moses' instinct at the burning bush, when he was compelled to remove his shoes because the very ground on which he stood was holy. And we see the same instinct in Isaiah's description of his vision of God in the Temple, when he was immediately filled with awe and an overwhelming sense of unworthiness.

The interesting thing about this

experience, from the point of view of religious argument, is that it is utterly useless in the Freudian or Marxist sense. The human being makes no use of it. Instead it calls forth from us an overwhelming urge to acknowledge a glory, to praise a beauty, to identify a distance between the human and divine that awes and overwhelms us, yet seeks communion with us.

The great souls who have written about their experiences of the divine all write differently, but there is a remarkable continuity in the elements of the experience they describe. Pascal's famous account of his experience is a good example. These words were found on a paper dated 23 November 1664, stitched into a lining of his coat and found after his death:

'FIRE. God of Abraham, God of Isaac, God of Jacob, not of the philosophers and scholars.
Certainty, Certainty. Feeling, Joy. Peace.'

The most interesting thing about Pascal's account is that he makes a fundamental distinction between believing *that* and believing *in*. He tells us that he experienced not the God of the philosophers, not the God that is a conclusion of an argument that may lead us intellectually to the conviction that God exists, but the God of Abraham and Isaac and Jacob, the God of people who trusted *in* the divine and took radical action as a result of that trust.

So the instinct to worship, to exclaim in awe, to praise, is the basic experience of faith. This is why worship together is the most characteristic activity of faith communities, whatever their conception of God is. It is true, of course, that experience of the divine comes to individuals, as the examples we have looked at prove, but it is also the case that the worshipping community is both a result of and a support for the individual's experience of God. If God is as we have experienced then the primary response is worship, giving due to God. It is undoubtedly true that we can worship God in private, in the garden, even on the golf course, and in a sense all human activity of any significance and value is an offering of worth to God. Nevertheless, intentional worship is a self-conscious act that requires practice and discipline, just as the maintaining of any important relationship requires time and carefulness. And true, appropriate and beautiful worship serves not only to express our faith but to fortify and deepen it, as we share in worship with our brothers and sisters and hear from them and go with them in their journey into God.

Varieties of experience

It is true that religious communities have often made too many claims for themselves and have set up all kinds of intolerable spiritual monopolies, but behind the excesses and overweening claims lies an ancient wisdom that points to the importance of the corporate. Just as none of us, even the most solitary, could exist without the support, often unseen, of the human community, so in our spiritual life we are fortified by others and the very way we talk about and experience God owes much to that great river of human experience we call tradition. So the wise person will have enough humility to learn from and join with others in the worship of God. And even the multiplicity of traditions of worship and belief have positive value. Undoubtedly human contentiousness and vanity have much to do with religious differences, but they do not tell the whole story. God is an enormous mystery and no single person or single tradition has a monopoly on divine wisdom.

The varieties of tradition point to varieties of divine experience. For instance, the varieties of religious expression within Christianity can be interpreted positively as well as negatively. Each tradition can be seen to emphasize or affirm a particular facet of the multi-faceted diamond of religious experience. In Christian history there seem to be four elements in the complex of Christian belief that are better held together but, human nature being what it is, inevitably get separated. The four elements are scripture, tradition, reason and spiritual experience.

Scripture

Scripture is the collection of inspired writings that are associated with the origins of Christianity. In Christian history there has been a wide variety of interpretations of these writings. They range from allegorical interpretations, in which the stories in scripture are seen as a kind of code which we must interpret in order to discern spiritual truth, right over to the opposite extreme, the literalist school of interpretation that treats scripture as the verbatim transcript of a live recording or original experience which is therefore understood as the literal voice of God, which is to be followed to the letter.

Whatever principle of interpretation is used, holy scriptures of one sort or the other are found in all faith communities and they provide an enduring focus for religious thought and discussion. For many believers it is this literary element in their faith that assumes the greatest importance.

Tradition

Associated with scripture is what we call tradition, the sum of the experiences of the religious community in question, as it has understood and interpreted its own history. Tradition, like scripture, is something that characterizes all human communities. Clubs have their rules and their written histories, but they also have a large amount of remembered experience that we call tradition. The word tradition means to hand on, to pass down the story, the experience, the memory. Traditionalists are people whose main focus lies in the preservation of the community's memories and collective experience.

Reason

In a kind of unavoidable tension with both the scripturalists and the traditionalists we find the group that loosely characterizes itself as rationalist or reasonable. Thinking about what we have received from the past, in written forms or through the collective memories of the tradition, calls for interpretation by the probing and questioning mind. This element, too, is found in religious communities, though with some people it gains an extra element of energy. Religious communities that stress the importance of reason are probably more characterized by fluidity and liberty than the groups that stress scripture or tradition.

Experience

And we must not exclude the living spiritual experience of believers for whom the faith is not primarily something based on precedent, tradition or their own reason, but upon overwhelming participation, often of an ecstatic and sometimes of a miraculous kind, in the present reality of God. Groups that emphasize this aspect of the life of faith are characterized by an infectious, if sometimes naive and undiscriminating, enthusiasm for supernatural activity in the community of faith, sometimes called 'signs and wonders', after the descriptions in the New Testament of the spiritual power that characterized the early Church.

Best together

The four elements that characterize religious communities are best held together, fortifying and modifying one another, but, since human beings usually find it difficult to concentrate on more than one thing at a time, there is an inevitable tendency for us to choose one of these emphases and make it primary. And there is even a kind of value in this, if only because it serves to underline the importance of each of the varieties of religious experience. There is strength, therefore, as well as weakness in religious diversity. At its worst, it divides believers into competing sects who claim that only they have it right. At its best, religious diversity allows for a range of temperament and response in religious communities that enable all the diversities of human personality to be at home. It is sometimes erroneously pointed out that it is this religious diversity which is the very thing that puts people off seeking membership of a religious community. This may indeed be true of particular individuals, but it certainly does not seem to be the religious logic of the United States of America, which is probably the most spiritually diverse culture in the world, yet continues to be a strongly religious nation in which at least half the population claims some kind of association with a religious body. All human truth and search after wisdom are a mixture of the good and the bad, and if we wait for a perfect expression of anything human we shall wait forever.

We have already seen that it is part of the perverse genius of human cynicism to stand apart and deny, rather than engage with and affirm the values of human or religious experiences. Some of this is probably due to fear and some of it is due to vanity. Neither is a good guide for the human pilgrimage.

The sense of unity

The second foundational element in the experience of faith is captured by the phrase 'a sense of unity'. The underlying meaning of this glimpse of the unity that lies behind the baffling multiplicity of creation is expressed in Mother Julian's famous claim that 'sin is behovely but all shall be well and all manner of thing shall be well'. That sin is *behovely*, or prevalent, points to the appearance of things, which is of division and conflict. Paul tells us that the whole creation groans and travails as though it were bringing something to birth. We must ask the question, 'Is this a chaos of meaninglessness and despair, or the coming to be of a new simplicity and unity?'

The vision of faith glimpses a unifying presence or principle, undergirding and infusing the perplexing conflicts of the universe. The focus of this vision is sometimes described as the *All*, the *One* or the *Other*. The experience of a real, though hidden, unity prompts true believers (that is to say, the ones who genuinely find reality and not neurotic versions of themselves) to a solidarity with humanity and with creation itself. The highest version, the most complete model of the true believer, is the saint, the holy or illuminated person in whom all barriers have been removed. Authentic religious experience enlarges human sympathy and compassion. It gives believers great hearts that are able to embrace the whole world in sympathy and generosity.

The demand

The final element in the foundational religious experience is the moral element. Recognition of the divine reality calls forth a spirit of wonder, a sense of the underlying unity of the universe and a feeling of responsibility, a felt obligation to respond in one's own life to the revealed mystery. This demand element is, inevitably, variously perceived and interpreted in religious tradition but its best essence is love of God and love of the neighbour. From this simple truth spin the intricacies of moral traditions and moral struggle, the attempt to be obedient to what we have seen. There are no easy answers to moral complexities but believers owe God the duty of moral seriousness in their life of faith. And this is not a question of reward, or fear of punishment, but of inevitable consequence. 'This being the way things are, this being the truth of things, how then should I live, what should my moral response be?'

Belief is for the whole person

It can be seen, therefore, that the experience of belief affects our whole being, heart, mind and will. Worship, joy in the beauty of God, captures our heart. Our mind is held by the sense of unity that undergirds the multiplicity of human experience. And the will, the active, executive side of our nature, is enlisted by the sense of moral demand that comes upon us as we say 'yes' to the divine vision.

But what about those who cannot believe?

Many of us may not recognize ourselves in any of this. We may be too hesitant and tentative to describe ourselves as believers, yet we are strangely drawn to the life of faith and wish we could own it for ourselves. Communities of faith should be big enough to include people like this, because the human experience of belief describes a wide spectrum that ranges from the ecstasy of the saint to the fumblings of the non-believer who longs to believe. The best and most generous communities of faith will recognize and allow for these realities. The best wisdom in the search for faith is to find out what we already believe and start there.

Rose Macauley, the English novelist, in her own constant wrestlings with faith, used to talk about an interchange of experience between hope, faith and belief. She spent a lot of time hoping it might be true; some time trusting, having faith that it was true; and the occasional moments of firm belief that it was. It was important for her to be able to bring all these phases of her own heart and mind with her into the Church, and fortunately she found that the Church of England was big enough to let her do this.

There are many rooms in the household of faith and there is quite a lot of movement between them. Being the kind of creatures we are, prone to self-defeat and cynicism, it is important to take some step, no matter how tiny. Sometimes it is a matter of nuance, of detail, a placing of slightly more emphasis on one aspect of our complicated life than another, a whispered yes to faith and a whispered no to cynicism. Many people stay with the whisper of faith throughout their lives, longing for that fulness of belief they see, admire and are nourished by in others. They, too, have a valued place in the community of faith and Thomas speaks for them: 'Lord, we believe; help thou our unbelief.'